A.R.
A.R.
Lex

D0853359

DISCARDED

5/89

A ROOKIE READER

ICE IS... WHEE!

By Carol Greene

Illustrations by Paul Sharp

Prepared under the direction of Robert Hillerich, Ph.D.

 CHILDRENS PRESS, CHICAGO

This book is for Greg and Marc.

Library of Congress Cataloging in Publication Data

Greene, Carol.
  Ice is—whee!

  (Rookie reader)
  Includes index.
  Summary: Ice is cold, slippery, pretty, and a lot of fun for children.
  [1. Ice—Fiction] I. Title. II. Series.
PZ7.G82845Ic 1983 [E]   82-19855
ISBN O-516-O2O37-4

Oh, boy! Ice!

Ice on houses.

Ice on trees.

WHEE!

Ice is pretty.

Let's skate on ice.

Around...

around...

12

WHEE!
Ice is fun.

Let's touch ice.

Oh, boy! Ice is cold!

WHEE!
Ice IS cold!

Drip, ice.

Drip on hat.

19

Drip, drip.

Drip on cat.

WHEE!
Ice is wet.

Let's run on ice.

Oh, oh.

Ice is...WHEE!

Slippery.

WORD
LIST

	let's
around	on
boy	oh
cat	pretty
cold	run
drip	skate
fun	slippery
hat	touch
houses	trees
ice	wet
is	whee

About the Author

Carol Greene has written over 20 books for children, plus stories, poems, songs, and filmstrips. She has also worked as a children's editor and a teacher of writing for children. She received a B.A. in English Literature from Park College, Parkville, Missouri, and an M.A. in Musicology from Indiana University. Ms. Greene lives in St. Louis, Missouri. When she isn't writing, she likes to read, travel, sing, do volunteer work at her church — and write some more. Her *The Super Snoops and the Missing Sleepers* and *Sandra Day O'Connor, First Woman on the Supreme Court* have also been published by Childrens Press.

About the Artist

Paul Sharp graduated from the Art Institute of Pittsburgh.
He has worked for the Curtis Publishing Company as Art Director of Child Life magazine.
At the present time he works as a free-lance artist at his home in Indianapolis, Indiana.